77 Ways to Celebrate Practically Anything

FANFARE

FOR A

FEATHER

Margolis · Smith · Weiss

Foreword by Ashley Montagu

RESOURCE PUBLICATIONS, INC.
San Jose, California

Editorial Director: *Kenneth Guentert*
Managing Editor: *Kathi Drolet*
Cover Design: *Adelle Weiss*
Editorial Assistant: *Anne McLaughlin*
Page Layout and Production: *Terri Ysseldyke-All*

Reprint Department
Resource Publications, Inc.
160 E. Virginia Street, Suite 290
San Jose, CA 95112-5848

Library of Congress Cataloging in Publication
Margolis, Vivienne, 1922-
  Fanfare for a Feather: 77 Ways to Celebrate Practically
Anything / Vivienne Margolis, Kerry Smith, Adelle Weiss
      p.   cm.
    ISBN 0-89390-202-0 : $9.95
    1. Rites and ceremonies–humor. I. Smith, G. Kerry. II.
Weiss, Adelle. III. Title.
PH6231.R56M37 1991
818'.5402–dc20   91-16134
                                                          CIP

5 4 3 2 1 | 95 94 93 92 91

"That which is not celebrated, that which is not ritualized, goes unnoticed, and in the long run those feelings and happenings will be devalued. The smallest events can be made into great moments of our lives by taking the time to celebrate them."

— Zsuzsanna Budapest, *The Grandmother of Time*

TABLE OF CONTENTS

FOREWORD

Delightful, whimsical, wholesome, reverberating with weathered wisdom, this happy product of three authors, whose combined age amounts to 225 years, is feather-light in the most practical of all senses, it is designed to lift the burden of daily living from one's shoulders, and assist the reader to revel in the ordinary challenges and occasions of everyday life as if it were a memorable occasion, with joy, with laughter, with playfulness, and charm, to take the ordinary out of living and transform it into the extraordinary, into a festivity, to confer completion, as the authors say, upon the event, that is the challenge to which we are called upon to respond.

E. M. Forster, in his novel *Howard's End*, again and again repeats the theme of his story with the words "Only connect." In a world in which we have been disconnected by Time and Space from each other, from our families, which are ceasing to be families, in which alienation and disengagement are the rule, and work, business, has become a way of life instead of a way of earning a living, in which the world of technology has outrun the world of humanity, it is more than ever essential that we should look to the restoration of our connectedness, to our authentic selves, and to a world which we *can* remake according to our heart's desire.

We do not know where the winds of genius may blow, but what we do know is that everyone possesses the genius and the spirit to transcend the daily circumstances of life and to transform them to achieve new planes of meaning and of joy. Toward that end *Fanfare for a Feather* is an enchanting contribution.

Ashley Montagu

March 1, 1991, Princeton, N.J.

ACKNOWLEDGMENTS

The authors are deeply grateful and appreciative of the contributions from family and friends

Rain	Amber Harris
Family	Charna Eisner
Lost Words, Almost	Peter Weiss
Sponge	Beth McGraff
Laser	Morris Weiss
Amber	Kathleen Smith
Spaghetti	Sara Weiss
Computer	Rob Ewing
Nose	Ken Guentert

INTRODUCTION

Celebration — we're all for it — and for the idea of finding your own reasons. *Fanfare for a Feather* was born out of the authors' collaboration and partnership in the celebration of everyday living. Our days together were filled with fun and play. We tried each celebration and found how easy and satisfying it can be to celebrate ordinary everyday things. Our awareness has become so acute that we respond to almost every little happening and see it as a cause for celebration. Objects, events, people, ideas, moods, and songs just seem to pop up and inspire us to rejoice in everyday things. The pleasure of a snowfall, a light breeze in the air, a special food, a reunion with a dear friend — move us to celebrate. We experience the extraordinary in the ordinary and go on to create a ceremony as a memory chip to mark it as important.

You may wonder why we celebrate both the computer and the typewriter. A contradiction? Not at all. More a matter of choice; the new computer for some of us, the faithful old typewriter for others. We collaborated on some of thecelebrations, while others, bath and collage, for example, reflect individual meaning. That's whysome celebrations say "I" and "my" and others, "we" and "our."

And then, celebrating *Shadow* "celebrations". How strange, you may say. *Shadow* is a common children's plaything, not for adults except as a Jungian term. *Fanfare for a Feather* reminds the adult reader of intriguing things long forgotten. There are other surprises, too. The celebration of Bath has an unexpected no-ending ending. This allows you to make up your own ending in the do-it-yourself spirit of the book, or, if you want, you can write to us and maybe we will tell you what it was.

Our emphasis is on excitement, humor, motivation, the well-springs of love, joy, tears, and affirmation of self and others. For celebration is all about feelings, feelings of empowerment, belonging, and sharing, feelings that confirm experiences and ceremonies to give form to those feelings.

Celebrations and ceremonies can be private or they can be shared functions, wonderful ways to make contact with family, friends, oneself, and others. They confer completion on any event. And, when you are the one in charge of celebrations, you realize that you can have them whenever you want. You don't have to wait for official holidays, a birthday, or a wedding to take part in a festivity. You can honor the moon, laughter, a special food, with a celebration and ceremony whenever you decide to have one.

Fanfare for a Feather is a book of celebrations that brings ways, means, and reasons to make something significant, tangible, and memorable. It invites the reader to experience personal feelings and sets the stage for the ceremony that follows. Ceremonies are sometimes funny, sometimes nostalgic, or quietly contemplative; all are designed to create awareness and remembrance.

We bring you seventy-seven items, each with its ceremonial pattern, the sparkle in the crown of that experience. *Fanfare for a Feather* is a resource for the young at heart. It casts an upbeat glance at what is often a difficult world. So we invite you to celebrate, to celebrate with a ceremony, to reach for a richer tapestry of life. We have our list for you to enjoy and choose from and we encourage you to make a list of your own. Rejoice, salute, sound the fanfare, beat the drum. Celebrate!

FANFARE

FOR A

FEATHER

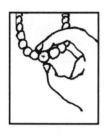

Amber

My amber necklace looks like half melted bits of butterscotch in dust filtered light from an Albuquerque sunset. Buried deep in one of the beads is a small winged insect. I cannot touch it, but see it like a miracle within. The body and wings are askew. Clearly some violence occurred in its capture, but its chief characteristics are perfectly preserved. When I look at this bead with its small captive, I can scarcely comprehend the immense number of days that passed before this fossil came to me. I am struck with awe and celebrate this silent, humble emissary from so long ago.

Ceremony

If you don't have an amber stone, try to borrow one, or use any other cherished stone. Keep the stone with you for 24-hours. Touch it, look at it frequently during the day. At night put it under your pillow. After 24-hours give it an extra rub or two and return it to its place. Close your eyes to recapture its beauty in your mind's eye, then thank it for its presence in your life.

Bagel

Celebrate the chewy deliciousness of a food that came to us from old Russia, and is now part of the American diet. It makes a marvelous teething ring for baby.

Ceremony

Slice a bagel in half and toast it. Place halves on plate surrounded by preferred topping (classic cream cheese and smoked salmon, or other kinds of cheese, jam, butter).

Raise one half high above the plate. Look through the central hole — see the world through your bagel!

Bring down, fill bagel, eat with delight.

Bananas

Beautiful yellow, lightly speckled bananas are delicious. Babies love them, school kids pack them in their lunches, young people cut them up over ice cream and under fudge sauce, and the older population can chew and swallow a piece of banana without hardship. The virtues of bananas are numerous: you don't have to wash a banana off before you eat it, it's sweet enough to serve as dessert, its shape is enticing, you can bite into it without worrying about the proverbial worm that sometimes shows up in other kinds of fruit. Imagine life on this planet without a banana.

However this wonderful fruit is used, it is always appetizing, and the only fruit with a Freudian complex.

Ceremony

With bananas, or your favorite fruit — ripe peaches, crisp apples, juicy plums, luscious cherries — whatever you are able to buy or gather, give a "Tom Jones" party for yourself and a friend or two. Sit opposite each other and feed each other the fruit of choice. Make sensuous sounds to enhance the taste delight. Wear a bathing suit if the fruit is juicy and if you decide to use a blindfold, it can add more fun to the experience.

Bath

When I was nine years old, my mother told me a story about her childhood in a little village, a "stetel" in Poland, and the bathhouse.

This bathhouse was the only place anyone could take a bath for miles around and then only once a week. Now that really impressed me. I had come to take the bathroom and the tub, the hot and cold running water, the electric lights, and the sunny window all for granted. I even had the nerve to complain about certain features; only one bathroom for the whole family, no shower like my friend, Gail had. I was expected to bathe at least three times a week, and if there were a ring left around the tub it was me, the youngest sister of four girls, who always seemed to be accused of the tell-tale disgusting residue.

Friday, the day before the Saturday sabbath was, of course, the most popular day for the villagers to bathe. Women and girls would line up early in the morning to be sure they got their turn at bathing. On one of these mornings my mother, then about nine also, stood in her usual place in line.

Just as she got to the door of the bathhouse, she heard the familiar barking dogs, an ominous sound because it announced the Russian Cossacks coming on horseback. They periodically raided her little town. In a split second, Celia, my mother, had to decide whether to crowd into the bathhouse and hide under a wooden bench, or to try to make it back to her house and the protection of the storm cellar where the family hid during such perilous times. Running home was too far. The horse's hooves pounding on the stones were quite loud now and so were the barking dogs. So Celia ran into the bathhouse. There were others in there – women hurrying out of the water, trying to put on their clothes knowing full well one of the cossacks could come in and snatch one of them. The naked younger women were particularly terrified.

Celia found a space under a bench in the corner. There were no windows, only the protection of the dark and damp space. It was barely a minute when a huge Cossack stormed into the bathhouse. He was brandishing his whip and that and his hissing sounds echoed from wall to wall. Celia was almost too terrified to breathe. Had there been even one barking dog present what happened next could never have taken place. This was a lucky day, the dogs had decided to continue running with the galloping horses.

All the women, clothed or not, and the bigger children too, like my mother, pushed the burly soldier into the bath water. Despite his strength and struggling, the women and girls held the cossack under water just long enough to weaken him.

That's when my mother would say to me, "After your bath you will hear the rest of the story." Needless to say, I hurried to complete this task as quickly as possible. Though I heard the end of this story dozens of times, it never failed to encourage me to love and honor my bath time which I do to this day.

Ceremony

You will need flowers to float, incense to burn, a favorite mellow musical tape to play, and a battery operated tape deck. Fill the tub with hot water, light the incense, float the flowers and put on the taped music. Step into the bath, slowly and carefully. Luxuriate there until you are ready to come out. Sing, moan, coo, hum if you want.

When the music has played through and you are ready to come out of the bath, close the shower curtain and take a quick cool shower. Listening to the water in the tub gurgle out completes this celebration.

Bed

I may not remember all the addresses I have had, the men I have loved, the children I have taught, or all the books I have read, but I remember almost every bed I have slept in, including the ones that were on the ground. An absolutely perfect bed, one that suits you in every way, the right length, the right hardness, the right width, the right temperature, and the right smell, with the right sheets and blankets is a locus of absolute surrender. Then too, the wrong everything can elicit such irritation and grumbling like no other.

A bed is a place where a kind of higher truth and soul searching takes place more readily than other places. It's a place to day dream, to night dream, it's an inducer of fantasy, an area of reflection, a reading space, a talking place, the realm of love making, a baby nursing location, a toddler bouncing location, a place to weep and a place to laugh, to reminisce, and to forget. A bed is a magic carpet to carry me places I'll never go and to see people I can no longer visit.

Ceremony

Find a friend or two or three or four or do this on your own. Get on the bed of your choice and spend time there recounting descriptions and stories about the beds you have been on. When you have finished this, spend the final moments chanting, "beautiful bed."

Bees

Without the honey bee, life as we know it would collapse. They carry pollen dust from one blossom to the next. They fertilize apple trees, pears, peaches, cucumbers, melons, most of all of our food and that of the animals as well.

What really fascinates me is the hive, a city of hundreds of "women" functioning harmoniously in a social and gregarious way, all intention focused on the good of the whole.

I never kept bees, myself, but I talked with a beekeeper once who told me to dress in light colors because bees find dark colors threatening; don't make quick movements but move with grace; don't wear leather, wool, or other animal products; don't eat meat for a day before you tend bees and never wear perfume or use fragrant soap. You see bees have an exquisite sense of smell and are strict vegetarians. I admire the bee. They really know how to express anger and are loyal to the death. Their prodigious work ethic yields the nectar of the gods. And if that isn't enough, bees see colors even better than humans do. They see both the visible spectrum as well as ultraviolet, which guides them to the pollen in the flower.

Ceremony

Pretend you are a bee and dance from flower to flower, preferably in your own garden, but a park will do. Gather some of the pollen from each flower and pass it to the other flowers. Buzzing a little will help you.

Bells

I wear a bracelet that has bells on it. One of my students who is blind greets me even though I am down the hall from where he sits before the class begins. He tells me that he loves to hear the sound of my bells when I move around the classroom. Somebody asked me, "Do your bells annoy people?" I've never had a complaint, but I guess that's because my bells are well behaved.

Ceremony

The next time you visit a friend, meet someone at the station, go to a party, manage to have a sit-down dinner by yourself or with others, gather up all the bells you own and turn that great metaphor "I'll be there with bells on" into reality.

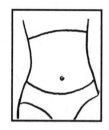

Belly Button

When I was little, I thought only I had a belly button. Then as I began to get older and wiser at the age of three, I discovered that everyone had a belly button; some with lint inside, some without, some turned in, some turned out, some red, some pale in color, but everyone had one. Finding out about this delightful part of the body was a memorable experience. The belly button continues to be awesome because it once held the cord of nourishment and life for everyone.

If you didn't have a functioning belly button for your nine months in utero, you'd be a goner.

Ceremony

Acting on the expression, "To contemplate your belly button," try it. Looking in the mirror, draw your belly button. If you have a friend who is willing to pose for you, draw that belly button. Next time you are at the beach notice the uniqueness of each visible belly button. Now you are qualified to wear the button "I am a Belly Button Watcher."

Blanket

Native Americans and babies understand the magical properties of a blanket. The baby coos and gurgles and drools over its blanket, clutching it in tiny fingers, sometimes rubbing the blanket-end over cheek and nose.

Nothing stops a baby's crying faster (other than Mother's milk) than "blanky" and smart parents never go anywhere without it.

The Native Americans weave designs into the blanket that give it meaning and magic properties. The blanket serves to carry important ceremonial items and once unfolded, the blanket is sat upon or used to catch a night-time dream.

My own blanket is such a source of comfort to me. It is my protector and loving companion, a trusted and beloved friend always there (unless it is in the wash).

Ceremony

Find your favorite blanket. Cover yourself with it an as many different ways as you can dream up. Smooth it, fold it, roll it, drape it, wrap yourself in it, play with it. Pretend you are a baby and use it. Then take a few minutes and write a little poem, an ode to your blanket or sing a little song, or just sit quietly meditating while holding your blanket around you.

Books

I'm addicted to books. Even when I go to the grocery store I tuck one into my purse, just in case. I swear repeatedly that I won't buy another and then, BINGO, I get a catalog and there on page 15 is an enticing ad for a new book. I simply must have it, and so when no one is around I take the phone into the closet, dial the 800 number and order a copy. I ask them to send it in a plain brown paper wrapper and preferably disguised, packed in a hat box. Sometimes I act as if I could give a book away. I magnanimously pull one off my crowded book shelf and force it on a friend who is trying to make a quick getaway. "I want you to have this book. Please, please take it. I loved it and you will too." Little does she know that I have a second copy hidden in the bottom drawer of my dresser. When I have heard her car door slam and her motor put-putting out of the driveway, I quickly put copy No. 2 in place on the shelf and heave a sigh of relief. My breathing gets easier and my anxiety has lessened. Once I thought about doing something about this book addiction. I looked in the phone book for Books Anonymous. There are no chapters yet. Maybe I could start one. Yet I feel I am not quite ready for the 12 step program when it comes to books. I'll start tomorrow!

Ceremony

From your own collection of books or that of the library, select ten books, each of a different size, binding, weight, and age. Place them on a table and fondle each lovingly. Then close your eyes and run your hand gently over each page of one chosen book. You can do all ten if you like to. When you are done, open your eyes and stack up the books on a table or nearby stool. Don't put them away for a day or so. Every time you pass the stack of books, run your hands over them, salute them, acknowledge them and when you are ready, put them back on the shelf or take them back to the library and do so with a murmur of love.

Boy

Celebrate the boy in all of us,
the rough and tumble part of ourselves
that wants to get into the fray,
play
in dirt up to our elbows,
shout and kick
and swing a stick.

Celebrate the quiet boy
thinking of how
he will climb mountains, explore space,
invent new wonders,
conquer his enemies.

Ceremony

Spend a minute or two moving restlessly about, swinging your arms and, if possible, giving a little whoop and holler. Then, very abruptly sit down quietly and note the difference. For a short time you have glimpsed the being of a boy. Honor and love that feeling in yourself and the next boy you chance to meet.

Breeze

Welcome stir of air
among the leaves and grasses,
nature's fan of summer
lavishing a cool kiss on our skin,
a fluff of our hair.
Stimulus to breathing,
the breeze lifts our spirits
and our steps as we walk,
soothes us when we lie looking up
into its movement among the trees,
delights us as it fills out the sail of a boat, or
    the length of a curtain.
Breezes are soft, moderate, or brisk. How
    well the name describes a breeeeze!

Ceremony

Make your own breeze with a hand-held fan or your breath expelled through pursed lips. Then hold up various light weight things and watch your breeze catch and play with them. See the paper, feather, leaf, piece of cotton fluff, threads of yarn or a chiffon scarf move and dance.

Chance

Who will trust their fate to chance? Who will celebrate the possibilities, good and bad, that fall on us by chance? Who would rather be bound by certainty, knowing ahead what can be known? Weigh the difference between these two and celebrate chance.

Chance lets us laugh with delight at surprise, adds an extra twist for a better spin of the top, pings coins into slot machines. Chance plays Pachinko with our lives — a lively tune.

Ceremony

Chant a Chance. While opening the refrigerator begin the chant, "Take a chance, take a chance, take a chance . . . " Get out an egg (uncooked) and a lemon (or apple, or orange).

Keep chanting "Take a chance." Now begin to juggle the egg and the lemon. Keep juggling and keep chanting. You can set a predetermined number of chants — ten to start with. If you get to 50 you can count yourself a lucky chanting chancer. If not, either your dog or a paper towel will auspiciously end the ceremony.

Circle

My favorite shape is the circle. Round, complete, and never-ending, it has no corners to stop the eye, no crazy complications like a pentagon or hexagon.

The circle is a delight to hold and behold. Circles are easy to make. You can trace around a dish to draw one or toss a stone into quiet water to stir up quite a few. I can't imagine how chaotic things would be without the trusty circle sometimes known as zero or the letter after "n."

Ceremony

Collect the circle shapes in your life.
Remember the Cheerio O's, the hole of a bagel or
doughnut, the period in the typewriter, the wheel
on the wagon, the pillow on the sofa, the ring on
your finger, the M&M's in your candy dish, the
beads in your jewelry box. Are there many more?
Make a list or just run down their names. It could
take several minutes of your attention.

Clouds

Clouds, ever moving, float and whirl across the sky, sometimes high, sometimes so low they seem to rest upon the horizon. They fascinate us as we try to read the message they bring with their arrival — rain tonight, sunny breezes tomorrow. We all love and dance with the clouds that appear like small sheep against a brilliant blue sky. And some share the feeling of dread and foreboding when heavy black storm clouds cover the dome above us. In every way we are grateful to the clouds for their drama, delight, sweep of grandeur, and for the blessing of their rain upon us.

Ceremony

Draw and cut out a few clouds from a sheet of paper. Give each cutout cloud a distinct personality and a name to go with it. Thus you may have "Stormy Giant," "Racer," "Swirly," and so forth. Tack these around your room for a bit of fun weather.

Collage

Ah, collage! How I love collage! I love holing up with a stack of old magazines and just leafing through them knowing that sooner or later I will tear out a choice picture. Then another picture emerges and another and another until there are dozens spread out on the floor around me.

Every once in a while I find an interesting article for a friend or one of my kids or for my own personal file of "wise sayings." When I am ready, I decide on the pictures for the collage and begin to cut, tear, arrange, rearrange, glue and mount. Sometimes I start with a dream as inspirational material. Most often an unconscious idea knocks on the door of my right brain and I put the collage together as if I were in a trance. It is a very satisfying feeling.

I have put together more than a hundred collages. I have them all in a box on a closet shelf. Every now and then I spend a few minutes looking at them. When I do, they tend to be reminders of my historical and psychological past, similar to a diary in a way. I can tell a story about each, and if you look at any yourself you will probably come up with your own story. Every collage seems to have its own universal truth.

Last week I went to a birthday party for a nine year-old friend of mine. I brought a large piece of cardboard, six glue sticks, lots of glitter, stickers, and scissors. We gathered the discarded birthday present wrapping paper, ribbons, and cards. I put the cardboard on the floor and in about an hour's time of fun and happiness, the birthday party participants had made a beautiful collage. The birthday girl had all her young collage friends sign the impressive piece of nostalgic handiwork. Then she took it to her room and placed it on top of her chest-of- drawers opposite her bed. Her father told me later that this collage is the last thing she says good-night to, before lights out.

Ah, collage! How I love collage!

Ceremony

Start a collage collection. Find scraps of paper here and there, shells, bark, stones, and other nature material, photographs, postcards, scraps of cloth, pieces of yarn, buttons, broken jewelry and other interesting junk, old greeting cards, magazine pictures. Then glue your collected treasures onto a piece of paper or cardboard to make your collage.

 # Collections

Collections start without your even knowing what is happening. The moment you are born people begin collecting things for you: booties, bottles, bears, beads, bunnies, and bells. It's a wonderful and comforting thing to have a collection. In fact it is archetypal; the collective unconscious, for instance. Better than anything is that moment when you find the perfect shell, the rare coin, the adorable tiny china cat, the missing 1935 National Geographic. Some people think only water, air, and a little food are needed to stay alive. Ha! Try it without a collection.

Ceremony

Get out one of your collections. Arrange and rearrange it. Stroke all the pieces. Ooh and ahh over each piece. Write a poem or sing a song to honor the collection, or just silently love it.

Color

Vibrations on the retina
in my body and soul.
Color speaks in many languages,
of love, delicacy, sex, and death.

How strange, a friend who is color blind
bought a gray car not knowing it was really red.
He wanted a color that wouldn't stand out, he
said. Then the car was stolen and the policeman
told our friend it was because the thief liked a
bright color. Naturally he thought the policeman
was crazy.

Color can make you happy, give you a
headache, stir you to action, please or displease
you. In all its brilliance and subtlety, color
permeates everything, surrounds and astounds us.

Ceremony

Take a package or two of multicolor construction paper. Lay out a path through your home. Follow the path. Take them up, shuffle the paper and rearrange the colors to make a different path. Invite someone to join you.

 # Commitment

There's power in pledging oneself to a cause, a thing, a friend, a partner, and know that one can sustain the commitment no matter what. A friend has been dedicated to anti-nuclear action for over thirty years, allowing nothing or no one to get in the way of that commitment. While relatively easy to pledge oneself to a cause, the care of an animal, tree, or plant, it's the commitment to people that's often the most difficult. Yet, the beauty of commitment is that it is bound up with love, understanding, and trust, responsibility, humor, and the acceptance of change.

Ceremony

Make a commitment to something or someone. Write it on a piece of paper and put it in a little box labeled "My Commitments." You can add these precious slips of paper whenever you decide to make a commitment. Then, one day bring out the little box and examine its contents or share it with a friend or loved one, or even an animal. When you complete a short-term commitment discard that slip of paper leaving room for a new one.

Computer

I call mine "Will," for Shakespeare, natch, and every time I boot up I say a respectful, "Hello, Will," and explain to him what we have to do that day. This may seem a little superstitious. But I came to word processing late in life, and it still seems like magic to me. Why take chances?

Word processing is merciful, that's why I like it. You don't have to sweat that last paragraph anymore, that fatal error that makes you grind your teeth and waste whole forests. Nowadays, you don't look nearly as clumsy as you are, without those little blossoms of white-out all over your pages.

Maybe soon they'll have programs smart enough so that you just outline your general ideas to the computer and it'll do all the gritty work of writing.

Until then, Will and I just keep tapping along, making errors of every kind. But you don't see 'em.

Thanks, Will.

Ceremony

Program "I love you, Will" (or whoever else you prefer) into your computer and let it go one hundred times or more. As the computer is tapping out this paean of praise, sing and sway along with the rhythm. Curtsy or bow to the computer and give it a loving stroke or two.

Containers

Celebrate containers and the mystery of
what lies within — a forgotten note,
a long lost toy, even empty
it holds the past.
Cartons, bags, boxes, tins, baskets,
buckets, bowls, vases, cases, pots, containers
all.
Everywhere we live, work, and play we find
containers.
Let's notice them, and
celebrate their right dictum that form follows
function.
It's even possible to put flowers in a case or
cook dinner in a bucket.

Ceremony

Place a row of at least five containers in front of you.

Arrange them into various categories — big, little — soft, hard — smooth, rough — pretty plain. Take time to realize how much you've taken these handy items for granted. Could you design a better container for any of the products in front of you? Think about it, then put all away where they belong.

Diet

If you eat something and no one sees you eat it, it has no calories.

If you drink a diet soda with a candy bar, the calories in the candy bar are canceled out by the diet soda.

When you eat with someone else, calories don't count if you don't eat more than they do.

Foods used for medicinal purposes never count, such as hot chocolate and buttered toast.

Cookie pieces have no calories. The breaking process causes calorie leakage.

Things licked off knives have no calories if you are in the process of preparing something or if you have been asked to taste something to see if it is delicious enough.

Ceremony

Breakfast: 1/2 grapefruit
1 slice dry whole wheat toast
1 cup herb tea.

Lunch: 4 oz. lean boiled chicken breast
1 cup lettuce
1 cup coffee
1 chocolate chip cookie

Dinner: 1 loaf garlic bread
1 large pizza with everything
1 large soft drink, your choice
Mint chocolate chip ice cream, not more than a pint.

Evening Snack: Frozen cheesecake eaten directly from the freezer.

Dolphins

I sat on the sand, spacing out, listening to the beat of the constant waves, when suddenly, quite close to shore, the dolphins appeared. There were 2 and 3 and more, nosing out of the water. I counted them calling out, 4, 5, 6, 7, 8. Yes, eight dolphins! Their grace and beauty magnified as they disappeared and then suddenly reappeared in a different place farther out. The dolphins swam in perfect formation ducking in and out, blowing jets of water above them, talking and laughing together like a bunch of school kids on an afternoon outing.

Ceremony

Sit quietly or lie down, anywhere: on your bed, while on a train, or waiting for a tardy friend. Let the vision of the dolphins come to you. Give them permission to come and invite them to give you a sign they are with you. Let them talk with you and tell you what they need and what they want you to do. See them as they appear and reappear. Finally, as they swim away, thank them for coming to you and then say, "Good bye."

Dust Balls

The room looked great and very festive, made ready for the Christmas party that afternoon, a Christmas party for the resident dust balls. These particular dust balls are my favorite little friends who manage somehow to come to other parties as uninvited guests. So this party is very special since the dust balls are the guests of honor. You never know how many will show up and which ones. I was ready for a big crowd. Sure enough the dust balls from under the table rolled out with the ones from under the couch. In no time at all the ones from the kids' room, the bedroom, and living room rolled out ready for the game, "Vacuum cleaner keep away."

Some dust balls are really expert and have never been caught. These old and wise dust balls really know how and where to hide and then just seem to have the timing down to perfection, dancing out to taunt me just as I have put the vacuum away. It's a great game.

Ceremony

Gather as many dust balls as you can find. Place them, with care, in a box. Take them outside and release them, watching as they dance and float away.

Eclipse

I've been an eclipse follower all my life. From the time I was a little kid looking through some smoked glass presented to me by my third grade teacher to this day. No matter where the eclipse of the sun is scheduled to be seen, I am there. I can remember one that I almost missed because the little plane I had hitched a ride in was not given the O.K. to land on the Island of Nantucket where the other eclipse freaks had set up telescopes and elaborate viewing stations for the big six-minute event. My friend, the pilot would not be deterred. He took his little plane down and made a daring landing on a sandy beach just in time for us to see the first dark sliver blank out the sun's rays. Then watch the event through exposed X ray film, the entire blackening of the sun, the feeling of the wind stirring the strands of hair, the evening song birds fooled into singing their evening melody, and finally the awesome silence, so profound that you hold your breath as you watch the breathtaking corona, a ring of light unique and solitary. That moment is worth the long journey, the concern that the weather won't cooperate, the worry that fog, rain, or clouds will obliterate the sun at the moment the moon moves in front of the sun and that it will last the precious hour or so of the entire eclipse. It is worth the time and effort it takes to mount the telescope and use the over-exposed photo film to protect one's eyes. All of it is worth it for that six or seven minute sight of the full eclipse. Now the tape runs in reverse and the sun unfolds, bit by bit, until the whole earth is once more bathed in sunlight. The birds are back to their normal daytime habits, and the viewer has been touched by magic.

There are, of course, eclipses of the moon, and they have their own beauty and enchantment. For eclipse thrill seekers, a moon eclipse or sun eclipse is where the action is.

Ceremony

Find out when and where the next eclipse of the sun or moon will be. Plan to go there even if the viewing is in the middle of the desert. Make all the plans and even if you don't go, you can pretend to go and on that day at the exact hour of the eclipse imagine you are being thrilled by the experience. You can find a photo of an eclipse in a science magazine or color one yourself and pretend you have taken the photo or drawn the eclipse as you viewed it.

Fabrics

I love the look and feel of fabrics of all kinds. I like to glide my hand along smooth satin, fondle the cushiony softness of silk velvet, enjoy the crisp quality of gabardine. I want to look at and touch everything from filmy gauzes to heavily embroidered brocades and tapestries.

However, while I am drawn to special and glamorous fabrics, I also admire and offer praise to the fabrics we use in our everyday lives. They are marvels of modern manufacturing and production. Sophisticated weaving (or knitting), and dyeing processes transform filaments of nylon and polyester and blended combinations into serviceable, beautiful fabrics that bring comfort and ease to our lives. They are both economical and practical. When we look back and compare our lives in this respect with those of the early American settlers we begin to appreciate how truly wonderful these modern fabrics are. In the Colonial era clothing and fabrics for the home were among the most precious possessions, gained for the householders through enormous effort and expense.

Ceremony

Whether related or not there are people and animals you call "family" with whom you want to celebrate. So gather any or all to a place under a tree. Send each on a hunt for twigs, leaves, nuts, berries, bark — whatever nature provides. When they return, dig a small hole under the tree just large enough to hold all the found treasures. Then sit down under the tree. Each person describes one item brought back. On the second round, each person uses the same description with one change. Instead of saying, "This leaf is beautiful, etc." the person describing the leaf will substitute "I." So the second description is heard as "I am beautiful, etc." After everyone has heard the second time, put the treasures in the hole and throw the loose dirt on top. Then family members enjoy a group hug and maybe even a group song before departing.

# Family

When my family comes to visit
We hug and kiss, and hug and hug.
Here there is breath.
Here there is life.
Faces that smile and laugh
And cry.
When we are together,
We are not alone.
When we are apart, we are still together.
We are connected through some inner force
That no one understands.
Inside each of us is the same seed,
Seed of death, seed of life.

Ceremony

Collect lots of pieces of fabric from your own rag bag collection. You can ask friends and family members to contribute. Place all the pieces in a paper bag. Close your eyes and put your hand into the bag, feeling the textures. Try to guess some of the colors and patterns. Bring out each piece one by one, spreading them out on a table. Now open your eyes so you can see the colors, textures, patterns, weave, size, and shape of each fabric piece.

Feather

There are many substitute person-made materials that seem quite satisfactory, but there is absolutely no way to make a feather. Only a bird knows how to do this: cardinals, wrens, parrots, chickens, eagles, even the tiny hummingbird has hundreds of feathers on its little body. And the way the feathers are designed to help the bird fly is so remarkable it makes our own featherless bodies seem quite ordinary.

When I go for a walk, I always look for a dropped feather, a feather a bird no longer needs. I have almost enough now to make a beguiling, fluffy, fantasy-filled, frivolous, fantastic fan.

Ceremony

How many ways can you use a feather? Find one and see what you can come up with. Perhaps a pen, a fan, a tickler, a head-dress. As a final tribute get out a party horn and watch your little feather friend dance and play as you blow the horn and sound a fanfare to the feather.

 # **Forgetfulness**

When I began to forget and actually remembered that I had forgotten, I realized I was having more fun. Now I can see a movie three or four times and each time the plot and characters are new to me. I am sought after by joke tellers, hearing even the very old old jokes as new and funny. I can read an article from an outdated magazine, and it appears vital and interesting. Sure I might have read it before, but it seems current to me. The leftovers in the refrigerator often stir my palate the next day as if the food had just been prepared. "Oh," I muse, "Where did this goody come from?" The adrenalin rush I get from trying to find my missing glasses or wallet gives me a sense of the excitement that I used to get when I played Scavenger Hunt. I feel lucky to have this opportunity to recapture my fun-loving ten-year-old self. Then too, the things, names of people and places I have forgotten usually return with a little jog. Now I have the choice to jog or not to jog. Some memories are best forgotten. It seems the ones I really want to recapture are close at hand with an old photo, letter, or story shared with a beloved. I look upon this time of memory cell depletion as a blessing no longer in disguise.

Ceremony

Tie some string around one of your fingers.
When someone asks what the string is for,
say proudly, "I forget and I'm glad of it."

Girl

Sarah is a five-year-old dynamo. She is beautiful, but it's not just because her hair is thick, brown, and wavy and her eyes a deep blue framed in thick lashes. She is a ball of fire, a jokester. She exudes creative energy and, what's more, Sarah can take charge of almost any situation.

One evening when I was baby sitting and having problems with her younger sister who would not stop screaming, I finally gave up. I left their room with Sarah in her bed reading and Isabel in the corner screaming. A few seconds after I left, quiet descended on the whole house. I returned to their room where both Sarah and Isabel were now happily reading in their beds. Surprised and puzzled, I asked Sarah, "What happened?" She answered, "I just told Isabel to SHUTUP."

That's what I mean, Sarah has a way. She plants her sturdy little legs firmly on the ground, uses a resounding voice, gives a clear direction, and with her quick wit, gets things done.

Ceremony

Write a limerick and send it to a child, any child from three years to 50 years will do.

For example:

No matter how grouchy I'm feeling
Sarah's smile is extremely healing
It grows in a wreath
All around her front teeth
Preventing my psyche's congealing.

Glasses

There's the kind you drink from and then there's the kind you see out of. I know the contact lens has just about outdated that trusty pair of eyeglasses you are always looking for. Still I notice there are plenty of people out there who are wearing glasses. The variety is exciting. I always see a pair someone else is wearing that I wish I had, like the pair I saw recently in the airport. They were purple polka dot frames set with sequins, lavender lenses and if that wasn't enough, they were equipped with a little button on the ear piece, which when pressed, activated something or other so the tune, "Deep Purple" played. And can you imagine, they were bifocals, at that.

Ceremony

Design and make your own outrageous frames using some colored paper, sparkles, jewels, stickers. Wear them in the house, at a party, at dinner, and if you are out for an adventure, to the grocery store on New Year's Day.

Gorilla

One of my favorite fantasies is to be held and loved by a gorilla. I fell in love with this magnificent, almost-more-than- human animal when I was twelve years old. Some girls of that age love horses, cats, dogs, birds. Not me; I loved gorillas. They were a secret passion. I was different enough from the other kids', to reveal this would have meant a trip to the guidance counselor's office. (They didn't have psychs in those days.) So I kept this love of gorillas hidden until today. Now that I am out of the closet I feel a lot better. I think that Jane Goodall would understand.

Ceremony

For part of a day become a gorilla. Eat, drink, walk, sleep, look as much like a gorilla as possible.

If you'd rather celebrate a different animal, go for it.

Handbag

Statistically, women live longer than men and no wonder. It's the handbag. If men only knew that the key to longevity lies in this simple inexpensive common commodity, it would change the balance of fortune. Not only that, men could join the ranks of those who mutter, "Where did I put my handbag?" or "Oh my God, I left my handbag at the restaurant" or "You kids, get out of my handbag." There is nothing like a handbag. It's an absolute necessity. To have only one is impossible.

There's the little blue one, the over-the-shoulder one, the red clutch one, the big straw one, the tiny beaded one, the one with compartments, the one picked-up on sale and never used.

It's practically impossible to get rid of any. I know. I have trunks-full.

Ceremony

Gather all of your handbags. Invite a friend to come and join you for a handbag luncheon. Inside each handbag stash something to eat or a little surprise, a sandwich in the red one, a cookie in the white one. When you are done lunching, perhaps you might want to trade one of your handbags for one of hers — not forever, of course, just, let's say for a month or so.

Kazoo

I saw a kazoo in a music store. It was expensive for a kazoo, $3.95. Of course that was understandable, the label read "Stradivari." I usually make my own kazoos from waxed paper over a comb. Lately I've been using plastic wrap over a toilet paper tube.

The kazoo is the most versatile and simple musical instrument to play. It makes everyone an instant participant in a musical combo. A three year old child can become a musician with a kazoo. When boredom strikes, I bring out my kazoo and amuse myself for quite a while. Its sound is not fortissimo, perfect for apartment dwellers. Even dogs seem to take kindly to its vibrating sound and will often join in with a howl or two.

The kazoo was first reported in the Lisbon, Dakota Star in 1884. Whoever thought up the name "Kazoo" was quite clever. When you say "Kazoo" and give it your all, it has the same vibrating sound that the instrument itself makes when you hum into it, a sort of noisy buzzing tone.

Ceremony

Either make your own kazoo or spring for a Stradivari. Spend some time playing your favorite show tunes, nursery rhyme tunes, or original compositions. Record a tune or two and you can use it on your answering machine. If at all possible, make enough kazoos for your family and friends and arrange for a concert time.

Kitty Cats

Most cats take as much affection and white tuna flakes as you are willing to dish out. Even the most indifferent and feisty cats are sometimes available for stroking, cuddling, and holding on your lap. Lately I've noticed that the popularity of cats is on the rise. There are cat clocks, cat books, cat cartoons, cat postcards, cat stationery, cat pillows, cat doorstops, cat calendars, cat dinnerware, and even a thirty minute audio tape that meows in different keys and rhythms to keep the cat owner company when the pet is at the vet's. Cats inspire loyalty despite their independent ways. "You can't live with them and you can't live without them," says one of my friends who has five cats, five cat bowls, five litter pans, five cushy sleeping places for her cat family. She should know.

Ceremony

Cut out pictures of kittens, puppies and other young creatures and use them to make a collage. Hang the collage behind the door of your bedroom so that every time you close it you will be delighted with these images that share your space. You'll fall asleep smiling.

Meow.

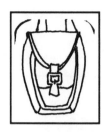

Knapsacks

When I was four years old I decided to run away from home. I collected some of my most precious belongings, a small doll, a few crayons, and lots of cookies. I looked for a bag or a box to put them in and there weren't any. Then I remembered a photo of a hobo I had seen in the newspaper. It was during a depression year and stories and pictures of hoboes were not uncommon. So I made my first knapsack from a scarf. I found a stick in the back yard to carry my knapsack and announced to everyone sitting at the dinner table that I was leaving home. I slung my knapsack over my shoulder and left.

Nowadays so many Americans of all ages walk around with knapsacks on their backs that we are beginning to look like a new species. Knapsacks come in all colors, sizes, moods. Time was when carrying a knapsack on your back meant that you were a serious hiker or intrepid adventurer. Now, if you're five years old it means that you're carrying primer and crayons to kindergarten. Thus your hands are always free to accept juice and chocolate cookies.

The latest derivative of the knapsack is the handy purse to wear on a belt around your waist. We will soon be invited to a museum exhibition of briefcases, vanity cases, attache cases, and "old fashioned" handbags.

Ceremony

Empty the contents of your knapsack on a table. Has it been a long time since you've seen that pen, and how about that old letter you were supposed to mail to a friend? If you do not have a knapsack, do the same with whatever bag you use to cart your treasures around. Same lesson. Knapsacks (and bags) eat junk.

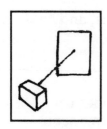

Laser

Celebrate the laser beam, an optical marvel. It pinpoints space, it comes in visible and invisible colors. Laser is Light Amplified Stimulated Emitted Radiation. It can melt metal, attach a retina. It is wondrous.

Ceremony

Read about how a laser beam is created and be impressed, even though you may not know how it happens. — and then recall the poem:

"Twinkle, twinkle, laser beam
How I wonder what you seem
All around the atmosphere
Neither far or neither near
Yet you can light up so high
Like a diamond in the sky."

Laughter

When it comes to living well, laughing is a necessity. Belief in its healthful restorative powers is fully justified. Norman Cousins laughed himself from illness to wellness. If you want to be and stay healthy, you need to laugh. Better than a lot of medicines, laughter is cost–free, revives you when you are tired, and makes problems seem easier to bear.

I have a little electronic device called "Freud's Anti-Stress Ball", that produces a laughing sound when it is pressed. I carry it in my pocket and when I travel it manages to start laughing at unscheduled and surprising times. I love it and am thoroughly devoted to its catchy message. Laugh and the world laughs with you, or do it just for yourself.

Ceremony

Gather things that make you laugh — cartoons, jokes, a laughing tape, Abbot and Costello film — and put them in a convenient Laugh Storage box. Then for a daily five minute or so laugh fix, take one out and use it. To spread laughter around, once a month mail a cartoon or funny story to a friend. Try this for a year or so. It will probably bring happy returns.

Light

Electromagnetic radiation.

Wave length from about 4000–7700 angstrom units propagated at a speed about 186,300 miles per second.

Something to see by.

Moonlight, a poet's inspiration.

Sunlight, a healing energy and a way to keep warm.

Twilight, a transition from beginning to end.

Light, we need and welcome it in our lives. There is the glow of a street lamp on a lonely dark road, the comfort of a lamp to read by. Then there are the dazzling fireworks that light up the sky leaving us breathless with delight, clapping our hands like little children. How often do we fail to notice dawn's delicate light or miss the drama of sunset at day's end? One man chose to watch the sunset every day for a year. He recommends it to those who cherish serenity, beauty, and light.

Ceremony

Sit in a completely dark room with your eyes open. Take your time and spend as much time as possible here. When you are ready, using a flashlight, send its beam here and there playing with the light beam on the ceiling, wall, floor, finding this and that, a door knob, table leg, tiny speck of dust.

Lost Words (Almost)

I couldn't believe it! "Kibosh," a perfectly good and useful word, practically unknown and in retirement now. It's a maverick word that our friend, Charles Dickens found useful in his story, "Seven Dials." Then Kibosh made a strong comeback during World War I in the song, "Put the Kibosh on the Kaiser." Kibosh is not the only word that somehow has gotten lost and longs to be remembered. Since resurrecting Kibosh, I have found myself using that wonderful word frequently and in new and unique ways. For instance, I suggest a kibosh break. I ask if anyone wants to go kiboshing. I go to the store looking for just the right kibosh. So here's to kibosh and all the other intriguing almost-lost words that can be found.

Ceremony

Find your own almost-lost word or make one up. Use that word in a letter to a friend, in a telephone conversation, at the dinner table, wherever you can for a whole day. At the end of the day write it on a piece of paper and slip it into a dictionary.

Magnifying Glass

We do not need microscopes to seek a closer look at the things around us in daily life. A handy magnifying glass will do. Look through it to enjoy the elegant symmetry of the inner parts of a flower. Use your glass to study the intricacy of filigree lace or delicate forms of jewelry. Use it as needed to read fine print, of course, but use it for so much more. I keep several around the house and reach for them often, the better to see you, my dear.

Ceremony

For one week, put aside five minutes a day to go about your house or garden systematically looking at everything through your magnifying glass. Don't forget fruit. Raspberries and strawberries are truly beautiful. What will you discover?

Monster

Monsters speak to something profound. They are about our shadow, a place in us where we can reach down to bring the demon out of the dark and into the light where it is not so scary.

Kids are smart about monsters. They can describe their personal monster in detail and explain its actions through incredible, bizarre stories, real and surreal at the same time. Monsters have a way of hiding under a bed, behind a tree, in a closet. Almost any dark, murky place is home to a monster. The best thing to do is to make friends with your monster and let it teach you what you need to learn. They are great teachers and can be wooed out of the closet by kind words or a joke.

Ceremony

Make a party for your personal monster.
Balloons, streamers, a welcome sign,
refreshments. You can keep your monster
invisible or make a large drawing of what it looks
like to you. I made a monster out of rolls of
newspaper using a large roll for each body part
and a ball shape for the head. It turned out to be
bigger than life size. I had great fun dressing the
monster and crayoning features on the head part.
My monster sat in a chair for quite a few days
while I got to know and love it.

Moon

Goddess of the night, she lures us with her mystery and beauty. All cultures observe and honor the Moon.

Following an old tradition in Japan, families gather just before moonrise to greet the Harvest Moon. They bring simple offerings and watch the moon with silent attention. When they speak they comment on their experiences of the moment . . . the color of the moon, the cool feel of the night breeze, the sound of the creatures in the night.

They write many poems about the moon. Here is one for your pleasure.

> The mirrored image of the moon shall be
> A pillow for the bird that floats
> Asleep upon the sea.

Ceremony

Select your own special day of the month to celebrate the moon. If you have a favorite phase of the moon, check your calendar to see when that phase occurs.

Stand quietly facing the moon.

Close your eyes, then open them slowly to fully absorb the image of the moon.

Begin to sway side to side. Continue swaying as long as you want, then come to stillness.

Bow to the moon.

Bid her a fond good night.

 # **Movement**

It doesn't take noisy exercise equipment at a spa or quiet yoga stretches in your living room to realize how wonderful movement is: even the tiniest movement of your pinky, your eyes, your toes, your nose, your elbow, is enough for you to know that "movement is life and life without movement is unthinkable" (Moshe Feldenkrais).

Ceremony

Stay very, very still, holding your breath for as long as you can. As you let out your breath move every part of your body. At first move the parts just a little bit, then move each part as much as you can — eyes darting, mouth opening and closing, body bending, arms stretching, nostrils twitching, fingers gesturing, and finally, make a clear and moving sound from the very depths of your being.

# **Mustaches**

A mustache is so much a part of an individual's appearance that it's funny to think of mustaches in the abstract. Full, narrow, fuzzy, neat, sloppy, shaggy, waxed — mustaches are many shapes and kinds as well as colors. Some men have hair and beard of a different color from their mustache. Some completely bald men like to sport a big, bold mustache.

The unresolved question about mustaches seems to be whether or not wearing one makes a man more attractive. Then too, there are cultures where mustaches are more common than in others. In the case of mustaches, ours is hopelessly ambivalent for there are times when many men wear mustaches, and other times when very few wear them. There are internationally famous mustaches — Charlie Chaplin's, Mark Twain's, and the beautiful snowy white one that matches the beard of Santa Claus.

Ceremony

If you have a mustache, give it your closest attention and respect today. If you don't have a mustache (and some of us women fall into that category) make one out of paper or draw one. Take a few minutes to contemplate your new look. Play the villain or the hero, the professor or the dandy. Does it move you to song, a soliloquy, dance, or a good laugh?

Nap

A nap is sleep, and more. It's at an odd hour, a time you choose, anywhere from five minutes to a whole afternoon, with or without music, in sun or in shade, on a rainy morning or windy afternoon, often alone, but not always. A nap is for you to savor and offers an intense refreshment of mind, body, and spirit. Some people talk about going in for meditation, a little rest, a quiet time, a nap-de-do just to disguise that absolutely yummy experience called a nap.

Let's face it, a nap is a nap, and it's the best.

Ceremony

Take a nap.

Native American

"This we know
The Earth does not belong to man;
Man belongs to the Earth.
All things are connected,
Like the blood which unites the family;
He is merely a strand in it.
Whatever he does to the web,
He does to himself."

Chief Seattle
Susquehanna Tribe, 1854

Ceremony

Native Americans have had for a long time the practice of gathering around a council fire to practice tribal wisdom. There each can speak freely of self, solve problems, or tell a story to improve one's connection to the great mystery of life. One of the most intriguing features has been the use of the "talking stick," which enables the holder and only the holder to talk. No one else may say a word during that time.

Find a smooth, thick stick. Gather a few friends and sit together in a circle. Put the "Talking Stick" in the middle of the circle. Whoever chooses to talk takes the stick. The ceremony continues until everyone who wants it has the opportunity to use the Talking Stick. It may take quite a little time, but it will be worth it to invoke the spirit of Chief Seattle.

Nose

The nose is fragile. It can be broken, catch cold, drip, get sunburned, and become clogged. What's more, the nose is nostalgic. Is there a pun here? Nostalgic comes from the Greek, nostos, meaning "return home." No sense stimulates memory like smell. Nothing brings you home faster than the smell of baking bread, the sweet fragrance of roses in the garden, or if you are a Gonzo exegete and farm raised, cow dung. Caution: the nasal memory is as short as it is long. You lose sensitivity to smells as soon as you become accustomed to them. Even putrid odors fade quickly. Well, maybe not the egg left rotting in the pocket of your summer jacket over a winter in storage. Freud's friend Fleiss considered the nose the most important sexual organ. Novelist Tom Robbins says that sex is eighty percent smell — that's forty percent for each nostril and even if one is clogged, that's not bad.

Ceremony

Take a day to notice noses. Pay special attention to the nose of each person you see that day. You may want to draw a few of the different noses — wide, narrow, hooked, crooked, turned up, turned down. Then look in a mirror at your own nose and give it a kind pat. For fun, add a noisy effect — sniffle, snuffle, and snort.

Onion

Black bread with a slice of onion has sustained many a hungry peasant and brought tears of happiness to his eyes. I must have been a peasant in a past life because the onion is a very necessary veggie for me. I need it for soups, salads, sandwiches, fried, boiled, sauteed, baked, or raw. I love its tear inducing aspect, giving me the chance to cleanse my eyes and soul. As protection against a cold a mouthful of onion prevents close contact with another person (unless the other person has also ingested an onion). And what a variety — green, spring, yellow, red, pearl — an onion to suit every aesthetic and gourmet taste.

Take away this translucent, succulent vegetable and your tastebuds will shrivel and disappear.

Ceremony

Using as many varieties as possible, arrange
onions in a bowl for a day-long centerpiece to
admire and appreciate.

Paper

There is nothing like paper. As you go through the day from the moment you wake up and read the news until you finally get into bed with a box of tissues by your side, paper is your trustworthy and constant companion. Just try to do without paper for one day and you will see what I mean: the computer could not print out, the writer, artist, and musician would be immobilized, without toilet paper the bathroom would be difficult to use. Beautiful Japanese rice papers, yellow lined pads, birthday wrappings, tissue papers, books, calendars, cards — paper deserves to be honored, protected, and cherished.

Ceremony

Using sheets of newspaper, wave them around and listen to the sound. Then make a lot of balls and toss them here and there. If there is another person present, have a newspaper "snow" ball fight. Tear some of the newspaper sheets, free form, strips, animal shapes, anything goes. Get out the glue and see what you can build using newspaper folded strips. See if you can make a compact newspaper brick and use that to build something with. Roll it, fold it, toss it, tear it, cut it, color it, cut it . . . . Check out its amazing and useful qualities for yourself. When you have finished having fun with the paper sheets, collect all you have made and recycle.

Pencil

We have finally come to the time when the pencil is an endangered species. Just yesterday I asked my granddaughter for a pencil. She handed me a ball-point pen, "Pilot B.P.S. Fine."

"No," I said. "I want a PENCIL. You know, it has lead in it and an eraser on the other end." She said, "Oh, a pencil. I've heard about those things. But what is it?"

Ceremony

Find a pencil, a very, very small one, an almost gone one. Mount it on a card. Put a frame around the card. Hang it someplace. Who knows, it may be worth a million someday.

Plant

The first thing I see every morning when I awake and the last thing that brushes against my hand before I drift off to sleep is my beautiful plant named Aphrodite. I named her that after I read *The Secret Life of Plants* by Tompkins and Bird. They said, "Short of Aphrodite there is nothing lovelier on this planet than a flower, or more essential than a plant." My Aphrodite almost decided to give it all up when after five years she had to be moved to a new home. I nursed her back to health with love and attention and two tablespoons of chicken soup once a day. Now she is grateful and loving to me as she sends me vibrations for restful nights and beautiful dreams. I love my darling Aphrodite with all my heart.

Ceremony

Pay special attention to your favorite plant (or plants). Notice its qualities and beauty. Touch and caress its leaves and stem while humming a tune or chanting "I love you."

Potter

A magic mound of clay
Giggling on the wheel
Then a pot full of laughter
Happiness.

Ceremony

Be a crafts person for a day or part of day.
Pretend you are a potter, a weaver, a paper
maker, a silversmith. It's your choice, and act as if
that is truly your calling in life. Go to a museum,
an art shop, or peruse a craft book at the library
or book store and pretend you are looking at an
art piece that you made. What is it like to look at a
handcrafted item as if you were the artist who
made it? What does it feel like to be a craft artist?

Rain

The drops fall lightly on the ground. As I lie in bed I hear the soft pitter patter sound and the quiet chatter. The crickets all around me sing a song like a symphony. The rain falls soft and long against the windowpane. I hear my mother creep in and say, "Good night my dear." As she walks out and closes the door, I curl up in bed and hear the rain drops fall once more.

Ceremony

Next time it rains deck yourself out in raincoat, rubbers, umbrella, and taking a lesson from Gene Kelly, do the tap dancing, knee slapping, vocal rendition of "Singing In The Rain."

Reflection

It was a window reflection that saved my life. Like most women, I am in the habit of window shopping especially when I'm in the Big Apple. Not only can you see the displays but you can see yourself — check out your hair, scarf, glasses — as well as check out others whose reflections appear as ghostly figures in front and in back of you. The mirror image I saw, that day just in the nick of time was a careening car making its way towards my reflection. So here I am telling you this story so you can know reflections for their practical aspects as well as for their intriguing beauty. There is the slow glide of leaves floating above the sky in the waters of a pond. Then there is that sudden surprise when I think the cat is out at night, but he really sits beside me. What startles me is his reflection in the glass door. Reflections bounce about, give depth where there is none, tease us in so many ways to our delight and pleasant confusion. And that clearest reflection of all, a well polished mirror fooling me into believing that's the real me.

Ceremony

Take a small mirror in hand and walk about in one room. Hold the mirror at all angles to reflect the many items in the room. Remember to hold it to the bottom of things too, the part you usually do not see. Hold the mirror up to another mirror and catch the intriguing multiplication of reflections.

Self

Your own song of self is written by you using self-love, inner security, and joy as the score. The song has sharps, flats, naturals, sometimes a tricky rhythm, a bass clef and a treble clef too. Learning to sing it may mean taking private lessons with a good teacher and lots of practice: practice of self-awareness, compassion, kindness, responsibility, flexibility, action. With all that, you become the composer of your life. You can beat the drum, pluck the strings, toot the horn in celebration of self.

Ceremony

A self — affirmation a day is the way. Sing it, write it, whistle it, dance it, say it. Remember those great oldies — "I Love You Truly, Truly Dear," "I Love You a Bushel and a Peck," or "The Best Things in Life are Free." Sing a chorus or a line of these or any other songs and dedicate it to yourself.

Shadow

I've had a lot of experience with my shadow. As a little kid it was often my playmate. Later I made and played with those amazing shadow ducks and birds on the wall opposite my desk when I was supposed to be studying. Then growing up to see shadows of leaves, buildings, mountains and feeling the poetry there.

It was when my Jungian therapist talked to me about my "shadow self" I finally realized the importance of a shadow and all the ramifications of that dark figure attached to my body, visible only with the help of a light source and sometimes big, sometimes little, sometimes not there and always an intriguing mystery.

Ceremony

Go for some shadow play of your own. Play with your own shadow, jumping, running, hopping, making it big and little. Have some fun tracing around shadows that appear on your wall inside or outside.

Silence

Ceremony

Shh!

Small Miracle

I was cavorting in the surf, feeling so confident that I neglected to take off my sun glasses. You guessed it. A wave caught me off guard, tore into me, dislodged the glasses from my nose and from behind my ear and in a flash the sunglasses were gone, carried to the sandy bottom and out to the sea on the next wave. I spent a minute or two feeling around the stony, wet, wild bottom, but to no avail. I sighed. I said good bye to the missing spectacles and hoped that some near sighted fish who needed bifocals would find them. Then (and here comes the miracle) my son went for a moonlight walk several nights later. He took a flashlight with him to watch the creatures of the dark scamper and dig their sandy homes. On the beach past the one where I had lost my glasses, he found my glasses, covered with wet sand but not a scratch or a bend anywhere. Now, that's a miracle!

Ceremony

Collect from everyone and anyone personal "miracle" stories. Keep a running account of each story, and make up a little book of your favorites.

Snow

As I watched the crystal — white snow pile up, I knew this day would be "cause for celebration." Why and how was what I didn't know yet.

I bundle up putting on all the paraphernalia for a snow day. I remember well, about 40 years ago, the large amount of energy it took to bend down and fasten my children's galoshes, slip on a sweater over a resistant head, stuff a well covered arm into a snowsuit jacket, try to find all the fingers that are supposed to fit into tiny size gloves and finally tucking curls under a little red ski cap. Oh yes, I forget the scarf. By the time all the clothes were on the children the snow had piled up another inch. Today, however, I have only myself to dress. I am ready to recapture the joy of celebrating the first heavy snowfall I know so well from my own childhood memories and then those of my children.

When I get to the sledding hill, there are already at least a dozen red noses attached to laughing and excited little kids who are climbing up a long hill, tossing snowballs at trees and moving targets too. They are screaming with joy on the way down the slope. "You wanna slide down with me, lady?" a nine-year-old asks. I am too cautious, too chicken, a bit afraid of a broken bone or bruised knee to accept his invitation.

The general excitement of the kids is catching and I am letting out whoops of splendid terror as I vicariously speed down the hill. With a little help from my mind's eye and inner voice I see and feel myself sledding down the steep hill and rolling off the bottom only to climb back up again pulling the sled behind me. I tune my sensory system into the sounds of the children, the look of the day, the feel of the snow, all that surrounds me. I am happy beyond words.

I have found the why and how of celebrating a snowy day. Putting together the now of my sensory world, the imagination my mind is capable of, the memory of the past, a celebration synergy results. I can capture and recapture when I need to celebrate the beauty, wonder, and excitement of a first snowfall.

Ceremony

Make a path in the snow, around trees, over hills and down dales, sprinkling bird seed as you go. Then wait quietly behind a tree and watch the birds have their celebration at this feast. While you are waiting, get out a magnifying glass and look at the snow crystals under magnification. Wow!

Spaghetti

See the spaghetti
dribbling down my chin?
I try to slurp it up,
but I don't succeed.
Reddish–yellow snakes
Aiming for my shirt.

Ceremony

If you don't know how to celebrate spaghetti there's nothing I can say to help you. I suggest seeing a psychotherapist, specializing in Pasta Phobia.

Sponge

Who was the first person to take that silent animal growing underwater and decide to clean with it? It seems an unlikely thing to think of while swimming — to think of cleaning countertops, kitchen sinks, and bathtubs.

Who thought of copying in plastic bright colors the sponge's ability to gather and relinquish?

Ceremony

Float a beautiful dry sponge in a nice bowl filled with water. Set a birthday candle holder with a birthday candle in it into the top of the sponge. Light the candle. Turn off the electric lights and enjoy.

Squirrels

Squirrels add frisky movement to the landscape. Usually they stay to themselves happily scampering through the trees until the fateful moment when you decide to hang out a birdfeeder. Then temptation is too much for them. They become thieves, thieves clever enough to outfox the foxiest and out squirrel the squirreliest. Agile, daring, aggressive, somehow, they always manage to get to the feeder or dump its contents on the ground for an easy feast. Clever creatures.

Ceremony

With paper and pencil in hand watch the next squirrel you see. Chart the squirrel's movements: up, down, across, loop-the-loop. No wonder they get away with so much. Stop and award the squirrel a moment of sincere admiration.

Stars

August is often the time of falling stars, and sometimes it lasts an entire week. In those warm summer nights the sky lights up and becomes wild with fireballs shooting through the darkness, leaving a blazing trail across the heavens. The astronomers refer to falling stars as meteor showers. No matter what they are called, I know you can wish upon that streak of light, and feel the magic of the moment that stars bring you.

Ceremony

Become a star gazer for a night. Pick one star and notice its color, size, position in the night sky. Talk to that star, sing to that star and give it a name making it your own personal star friend. Then make a wish upon it.

Stick

It wasn't until recently when I had to find a helping walking stick to get me home safely on a slippery wooded path that I began to recount all the necessary sticks that had been in my life.

Starting with the wondrous, smooth interlocking sticks, called Tinker Toys I played with while recovering from a tonsillectomy as a child; the shiny sharp stick my piano teacher used across my knuckles to discipline my uneducated hands to play the right notes; the favorite stick I used to play street hockey; the first chop sticks that mystified me at a Chinese restaurant; the gnarled sticks I collected as a teen-ager on romantic walks in the woods; the sticks I kept under my pillow as wishing sticks; the I Ching sticks playing wise oracle; the little important sticks I gathered to start a campfire or use in the indoor fireplace when a storm had broken the power lines and there was no heat or light in my home; the newspaper sticks I learned to make when I couldn't find wooden sticks; and now the pick-up-stick game I play with my grandchildren.

Ceremony

Find a favorite stick. Meditate on it and when you are ready write a sentence or two or even a haiku about this wonderful, useful, and beautiful bit of nature.

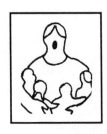

Story

a story animates your being
a story needs a voice
a story wants to be heard
a story comes to live in you
inhabiting you like your own life force
a story traps the past and predicts the future
a story amuses, bemuses, surmises, and
    tantalizes
a story is part of a universal dream.

Tell me your story
And I'll tell you mine.
Tell me a story that will scare me
Or surprise me.
I'll tell you one that will make you sad.
Tell me a funny story,
I like them best of all.
Tell me a story of long ago.
Let me tell you one about the future.
Tell me a story about space men
Or cave dwellers.
Now that we've heard all these stories,
Let's celebrate and find someone else
To tell them to.

Ceremony

Find a story you like — Three Billy Goats Gruff, Beauty and the Beast or an O'Henry story. Read it to someone or record it on tape and listen to it yourself. When you are ready, make up a story of your own.

Sun

Once upon a time, many thousands of years ago, there lived a beautiful and powerful Amazon woman. She had long, thick flowing red hair, dark green eyes, and skin as translucent as the moon. Her faithful companion, a snow leopard, was also strong and beautiful. She was happy and proud to serve the Amazon Woman as her faithful friend and ally. Together Amazon Woman and Snow Leopard spent their days healing the earth and their nights healing the animals and people. As you might guess, they were very, very, busy. Though not as busy as they would be now.

One morning as they were about to begin a new day, they greeted their friend the Sun with their usual good morning sun song. The sun smiled a sunny smile, winked his sunny eye, and with his sunny mouth said, "Thank you, Amazon Woman and Snow Leopard. I invite you, friends, to come and live with me. Come and use my energy for your healing powers. You will have even more time to play and have fun in the sun."

So from then on, Snow Leopard and Amazon Woman lived with their friend Sun, and to this very day Snow Leopard, Amazon Woman, and Sun help heal the earth, people, and animals.

Ceremony

On a very sunny day, go outside or stand in front of a sun-filled window and make up your own particular "salute" to the sun, bending and swaying with outstretched arms, perhaps, or humming or chanting or doing whatever feels sunny.

T-Shirt

At first only babies and men wore T-shirts, in that order. Somehow, somewhere, at some time or other a T-shirt became something to define one's politics, interests, persona, sense of humor, philosophical values, religious beliefs, and sexual persuasion. I know people who collect T-shirts as some people collect coins and may have as many as a hundred different T-shirts from foreign countries that don't even exist anymore. I read once that Jacqueline Kennedy had about 200 T-shirts, one for every kind of state occasion and then some. I have about fifteen T-shirts at last count. Of course, some are a bit stained, too small, the message no longer pertinent, the color faded, a hole here or there, but I just can't get rid of any. "A Good T-shirt Never Dies" is a motto written on one of them.

Someone told me that by the year 2000 the T-shirt fad will be replaced by some other ordinary piece of clothing such as socks. I don't think so. There simply isn't room on socks to print the kind of slogans I see on T-shirts: for instance, the explanation of the theory of relativity, the first movement of the Moonlight Sonata. The T-shirt is here to stay, and I bet it will be a hot item in the first outer space mall.

Ceremony

Take out all your T-shirts and arrange them lovingly on your bed. Before you put on your favorite one, sing "Happy Anyday to you."

Tears

Tears are
The purest liquid excreted from your body
The voice of the soul
The message from the heart
A healing balm
The Tao of clarity

Ceremony

"Enjoy a good cry," a great cliche. So do it. Just close your eyes. Think of someone you love or have loved and who is no longer in your life. See that absent loved one and see yourself going to him/her. Tell that person how much you love and miss her/him. Even if the tears don't well up, the heart's feelings are tearful message enough.

Tools

Celebrate the tools you use — the handy hammers prepared for anything, pocketknives, screwdrivers in all sizes, special scissors for all purposes. You must have a few of your own to celebrate. Do you have an awesome awl, practical pliers, or other toothsome tools? Lay out your collection on a table. Think of all the ways you use each tool.

Ceremony

Choose your favorite tool, one you use most often. Wrap it up carefully and put it away with a sign on it, "DO NOT TOUCH." When you need it and absolutely can't do without it another minute, find it. Unwrap it, stroke it, and from your heart murmur, "I missed you."

# Trains

I take a train almost everywhere: into the Big Apple, through city tunnels, under water and across bridges. Their inconvenience only serves to make them more of a challenge. Will I get a seat? Will the train cars be cold and drafty or worse, stifling hot? Is ptomaine poisoning part of the tuna fish sandwich? Will my seat be broken and refuse to stay in an upright position or will it jerk back when I least expect it?

Yet I go out of my way to schedule my traveling life around the train schedule loving the sound of the turning wheels, the rocking motion as it speeds along, the fast moving scenery outside the dirty windows, my own reflection there to keep me company, the person who tumbles in your lap as he is making his way to the rest room, the people reading, sleeping, talking, arguing. It's a trip all right.

Ceremony

Go to a train station and buy a round-trip ticket to the next stop. On this trip become familiar with the smells, sounds, texture of the seats. Walk up and down the aisle. Walk through all the cars from one end of the train to the other. Then before you are ready to depart, write a little greeting and leave it on the seat for the next person who will occupy it.

Typewriter

I've seen the truth — and it's my old reliable, familiar, well-used typewriter. The click of the keys, the ring at the end of the line, the ingrained smudges from typo-erase, the slowness that allows me to gather my thoughts. My computer friends tell me that I could write much faster on an Apple. Well, I still think that an apple is for eating, and who needs to write so fast anyway?

My typewriter is like a musical instrument to me, an old Strad that keeps getting better and better as time goes on. I bet that if I could use Shakespeare's pen I might be totally inspired. The same goes for the typewriter that Hemingway pounded. That's another thing — I really have to pound to get my machine to move along — and this action brings excitement and creativity as well.

Maybe when I am very old I will buy a computer instead of a rocking chair so I can have something to sit in front of and play with. On second thought though, a rocking chair will give me some much needed movement and an opportunity to dream.

Ceremony

Find an old typewriter. You may have to locate a store that still carries them. There are probably some old Hermes and Remingtons around. Notice the case, the color of the machine, the sound of the keys as they are pressed. Then try them out, typing an ode or poem to this almost obsolete machine of the not-so-distant past.

Umbrella

Is an umbrella something to value, to cherish, worthy of consideration? Ask me when I get caught in a downpour without one. Or when I am at the beach, let me know how to shield myself from the hot sun without an umbrella.

On the other hand, when I have an umbrella with me and I need one, I pop it open without a thought, casual as can be.

And all those lost umbrellas, hiding in unfamiliar places: restrooms, libraries, bus and train stations, waiting rooms in foreign countries.

If my umbrella gets lost I want its final resting place to be in a church or temple, a place that suits such a trusty friend.

Ceremony

Get out your umbrella. Put some dancing music on your tape deck or radio. With your umbrella closed, use it as your dance partner, waltzing, doing the rumba, jitter-bugging. When you open it, dance again.

Walking

Walking seems like such a simple thing to do. You put one foot in front of the other and somehow the body does this "no big deal" thing and goes right along as if it were as easy as ABC. You need only watch the one year old new walker to realize the amazing coordination it takes to learn how to walk.

The greatest walker in our family was my great grandfather. In 1828, hearing about lots of rich land in the Louisiana Purchase, free to homesteaders, he and his young wife "went west." Having very little money, he borrowed a horse from a neighbor for his pregnant wife to ride the thousand miles from Tennessee to Missouri while he walked alongside. Since he always returned property, he rode the horse back to its owner and then walked the thousand miles home to Missouri.

A year or so after my great grandfather's daughter, Eliza Jane, was born they decided to move back to Tennessee. Again he borrowed a horse from a neighbor and he walked the thousand miles beside the horse that was carrying his wife and baby daughter. Of course, his honor compelled him to take the horse back to its owner in Missouri. And, of course, there followed his fourth thousand-mile walk, back to Tennessee. They had been gone just a little over two years. During that time my great grandfather had walked 4000 miles and his young wife had covered 2000 on a borrowed horse.

Ceremony

Next time you are out on a walk try all the different kinds of walks you have seen and heard of including some of the times you played "Mother-May-I." There's the scissors walk, the elephant walk, the baby steps, the backward walk, and the one that looks as if you are Charlie Chaplin.

Watch

I really never thought how important watches had become until I saw an ad for an Andy Warhol watch, costing $1800. The face pictures a tomato soup can and, of course, there are no numbers. Come to think of it I didn't see any hands either. Well, who cares? Watches are an art form, a status symbol, a necessary accessory that must match the outfit.

I had a pretty groovy watch with a matching plastic band. It cost only $15.95, but it was a great watch. Then the plastic band wore out and since it was permanently affixed to the watch that was the end of it. I didn't get another. I decided to go back and use my 30-year-old Mickey Mouse watch with the life-time metal band, not permanently affixed. It already has senior citizen status and is still as good as new. You can tell the time by it too, and it has a comforting little tick when you keep it wound.

Ceremony

Find an old cheap watch in a thrift store or maybe you have one around that doesn't work anymore. Take it apart using one of those tiny jeweler's screw drivers. Notice the beauty of the parts. Use them in a construction or a collage that pays homage to the watch.

Weeds

Try not to be disdainful towards weeds. Survivors and outcasts, they need and deserve our notice and respect. What's more, upon closer examination you can find them quite attractive; some even have lovely blooms. One person's weeds can be another person's flowers.

Ceremony

Pick a bouquet of weeds for your kitchen table. Now substitute the word "flower" for "weed" and give each part of your bouquet a beautiful new name. Write the new name or names on a card and place it near the bouquet. While you gaze on this simple and innocent arrangement, welcome each "flower" with its new name.

Window

When I had to work in a room without a window, I soon realized that having a window can be cause for celebration:

The seat by the window in a train, plane, or automobile.

The window in the bathroom that can be opened when necessary.

The sunny window and its sill for your geraniums.

The odd-shaped window in the attic.

Stained glass window in the church or synagogue.

The frosted window in the winter.

The sound of rain against the window in the summer.

The window that invites daydreams in the classroom.

The sparkling just-washed window.

The open window that lets in the cool summer breeze.

My mother told me, "Your eyes are the windows to your soul."

Ceremony

Using some Bon Ami, make a thick paste. Dip your finger in it and draw or write on one of your windows covering it completely. Then with a soft cloth, a crumpled piece of newspaper, or paper towel, wipe the window clean. Spend a moment or two with just you and your window.

Kerry Smith, Ph.D. joined the U.S. Department of Education before heading the American Association for Higher Education. He created the Teacher of the Year Program, the weekly network, "Meet the Professor," and aided in establishing the Federal Student Loan Program. Now 86, Smith specializes in psychoneuroimmunology, as well as assorted daily fanfares.

Vivienne Margolis, Ph.D. is a teacher, psychotherapist, collage artist, and self-appointed Grandma of the year for the past twelve years. You can find her swimming in the morning, listening, laughing and crying with clients in the afternoon, and reading, writing, and celebrating in the evening. She is the co-author of four other books, two with Adelle Weiss.

Adelle Weiss, artist and author, lives with her husband and fifteen pound cat in Cape Cod, Massachusetts. She enjoys printmaking and painting and is a member of the Harwich Arts Council and other artist's organizations. This is her third collaboration with Vivienne Margolis.

FEEDING THE SPIRIT: How to Create Your Own Ceremonial Rites, Festivals, and Celebrations

Nancy Brady Cunningham

Paperbound, $7.95
118 pages,
5½" x 8½"

ISBN 0-89390-117-2

Combine ancient rites and modern-day practicality with these 24 ceremonies you can celebrate in your home.

Ceremonies such as Dream Making, Color Meditation, and Moon Magic will inspire you to create your own rituals; the solstice and equinox celebrations will add a special air to each season.